# How to Reach Your Favorite Sports Star

### Revised Edition!

▼▼▼▼▼

# How to Reach Your Favorite Sports Star

## Revised Edition!

▼▼▼▼▼

*by*
*Larry Strauss*
*and Hal Unterberger*

**Lowell House Juvenile**
**Los Angeles**
• • • • • •
**Contemporary Books**
**Chicago**

Publisher: Jack Artenstein
Vice President, Juvenile Division: Elizabeth D. Amos
Director of Publishing Services: Rena Copperman
Editorial Director: Brenda Pope-Ostrow
Senior Editor: Amy Downing
Editorial Assistant: Jessica Oifer
Art Director: Lisa-Theresa Lenthall

Library of Congress Catalog Card Number is available.

ISBN: 1-56565-301-7

10 9 8 7 6 5 4 3 2 1

# Reach out and touch your favorite star!

*I*f you've ever had the impulse to tell a special sports celeb exactly how you feel, grab a pen and do it now!

But how do you reach your favorite sports stars? It's easy. Read about them in the following pages, then write to the addresses that accompany each entry. For best results, remember the following:

➤ Don't obsess about spelling, grammar, and/or sounding foolish. These are fan letters you're writing, not English compositions. Remember to have fun!

➤ If you want a reply, it's best to send a self-addressed, stamped envelope (SASE) along with your letter. That's an envelope with a first-class postage stamp and your name and address printed legibly on it.

➤ If you are writing to or from a country other than the United States (for instance, if you are in Canada writing to a star at a U.S. address), you will need to include international postage coupons with your letter. You can purchase international postage coupons at any post office.

➤ Sports stars change addresses and teams just like anybody else. But even if the person you write to is long gone, your letter should be forwarded to his or her new address.

# Contents

▼▼▼▼▼▼▼▼▼▼▼▼▼▼▼▼▼▼▼▼▼

# Jim Abbott

*I*n the strike-shortened season of 1994, pitcher Jim Abbott accomplished something many thought virtually impossible: He pitched a no-hitter! If the season had been completed, one can only imagine how great Jim's year might have been. Why was this feat especially impressive? As many baseball fans already know, Jim is the first major league pitcher in history with only one hand. This has been a source of continual amazement and a reason why Jim is so admired for his skill as a ballplayer. He has taken his disability and gracefully turned it into a personal triumph.

## Cool Credits

➤ Most Valuable Player of University of Michigan baseball team, 1988
➤ Big Ten Conference MVP, 1988
➤ Olympic gold medal (pitched gold medal game against Japan), 1988
➤ Topp all-rookie selection, 1989

## Vital Stats

➤ Height: 6'3"
➤ Weight: 210
➤ Birthplace: Flint, Michigan
➤ College: University of Michigan
➤ Current residence: Newport Beach, California
➤ Favorite athletes: Nolan Ryan, Alan Trammell, and Orel Hershiser

➤ Favorite food:
Mexican
➤ Ambition after
baseball: to be a
writer

## Birthday Beat
*September 19, 1967*

### So You Want to Know—

How far Jim's popularity extends? As much as he is adored by American baseball fans, nothing compares to the adulation he received in Cuba. In July of 1987, Jim pitched for Team USA in Cuba against the Cubans, who were then considered the best amateur team in the world. He pitched a three-hitter and won the game 8–3. It was the first U.S. win over Cuba in twenty-five years! After the game, thousands of Cuban citizens treated Jim like a national hero.

Jim Abbott
c/o The Chicago White Sox
New Comiskey Park
333 W. 35th St.
Chicago, IL 60616

# Andre Agassi

## Cool Credits

➤ U.S. Clay Court Championships winner, 1988
➤ Top 10 ranking, 1988–1993
➤ French Open finalist, 1990, 1991
➤ Wimbledon winner, 1992
➤ Davis Cup winning team, 1992
➤ U.S. Open winner, 1994
➤ Australian Open winner, 1995

## Vital Stats

➤ Height: 5'11"
➤ Weight: 175
➤ Birthplace: Las Vegas, Nevada
➤ Current residence: Las Vegas, Nevada
➤ Favorite food: Italian
➤ Favorite way to travel: flying on his own private jet
➤ Favorite actress: girlfriend Brooke Shields

## Birthday Beat
*April 29, 1970*

*A*t the age of sixteen, Andre hit the professional courts as a new young sensation, defeating players twice his age. Back then his father, Mike Agassi, was the driving force behind his success, always there to remind Andre when it was time to practice, what to do, and what not to do. Even when Andre won matches, his dad would point out the weaknesses in his game so that his son would get better. Now Andre is all grown up and has matured into one of the greatest tennis players of all time, and he hasn't had to depend on his father to push him.

### So You Want to Know—

How Andre spends some of the dough he makes? He is very generous and takes care of those people who have looked out for him. He bought his parents and his business partner homes. He even bought a new car for his business partner's daughter on her sixteenth birthday!

Andre Agassi
Agassi Enterprises
2300 Sahara Ave., #1150
Las Vegas, NV 89102

# Troy Aikman

When the Dallas Cowboys drafted 22-year-old Troy Aikman from UCLA, few realized that within only three seasons Troy would lead the Cowboys to back-to-back Super Bowl victories. Troy is one of the smartest quarterbacks in the game. He carries a laptop computer with him on the road to study opposing defensive statistics, and in the game he is known to make very few mental errors. He has great mobility behind the line of scrimmage and hardly ever gets sacked. His arm is strong and his passes are almost always right on target. While some feel he is already at the top of his game, he seems to just keep getting better and better.

## So You Want to Know——

How deep Troy's "cowboy" roots go? Troy may be a Dallas Cowboy during the football season, but he's actually an Oklahoma cowboy at heart. His roots are in Henryetta, Oklahoma, where his family moved when he was twelve. In Oklahoma he's known as a laid-back, down-to-earth cowboy who wears boots and drives a GMC Yukon truck. "I'm proud of my upbringing," he says.

## Cool Credits
➤ NCAA all-American, 1989
➤ First NFL draft pick, 1989
➤ Selected for the Pro Bowl for four consecutive seasons, 1991–1994
➤ Led Cowboys to two consecutive Super Bowl victories, 1993, 1994
➤ Has the highest quarterback rating (111.2) in NFL playoff history

## Vital Stats
➤ Height: 6'4"
➤ Weight: 228
➤ Birthplace: West Covina, California
➤ College: University of California, Los Angeles
➤ Current residence: Irving, Texas
➤ Nickname: T-Roy
➤ Leg strength: can lift 640 pounds with his legs!
➤ Favorite food: Italian
➤ Idol growing up: basketball star Larry Bird

## Birthday Beat
*November 21, 1966*

Troy Aikman Fan Club
P.O. Box 201326
Arlington, TX 76011

**13**

# Amy Alcott

■ ■ ■ ■ ■ ■ ■ ■ ■ ■ ■ ■ ■

*A*t only five-and-a-half-feet tall, Amy Alcott may not have the power of many of the female golfers she competes against, but she's one of the most accurate players on the course. In fact, for pure accuracy of shots, Amy may be the best female golfer in the world. She needs only one more tournament victory to become the thirteenth female golfer to make it to the Pro Golf Hall of Fame. While she's a fantastic player, Amy already has retirement plans—to study golf course architecture and design. She also looks forward to one day being able to travel and play golf, without worrying about defeating the best players in the world.

## Cool Credits

➤ Won the Nabisco Dinah Shore Tournament three times in her career, 1983, 1988, 1991

➤ Won the LPGA National Pro-Am, 1986
➤ Recorded six Top 10 placings, 1989
➤ Has won twenty-nine LPGA (Ladies Professional Golf Association) tournaments in her career

## Birthday Beat
*February 22, 1956*

## So You Want to Know—

What Amy does with her spare time? She has her own charity golf tournament to benefit the Multiple Sclerosis Society. The Amy Alcott Pro-Am for Multiple Sclerosis has raised over $750,000. She has also made several golf scholarships available for high school golfers who wish to attend UCLA.

## Vital Stats

➤ Height: 5'6"
➤ Birthplace: Kansas City, Missouri
➤ Current residence: Santa Monica, California

➤ Joined LPGA: 1975
➤ Low career round: sixty-five
➤ LPGA career holes-in-one: three
➤ Major influence: golf pro Walter Keller
➤ In her spare time: works as a baker at the Butterfly Bakery in Los Angeles
➤ Favorite food: baked goods

Amy Alcott
c/o LPGA Headquarters
2750 W. International Speedway Blvd.,
Suite B
Daytona Beach, FL 32114

15

# Roberto Alomar

ots of fathers and sons play ball together, but Roberto Alomar and his brother, Sandy, Jr., did it playing on a major league team. In 1985, their father, former major leaguer Sandy Alomar, Sr., was hired as a coach for the San Diego Padres, the same team that both Roberto and Sandy, Jr., were playing for.

At the time, baseball scouts praised Sandy, Jr., for his skills. Since then, second baseman Roberto has proven that he is the more gifted of the two talented Alomars. In 1990, Roberto was traded to the Toronto Blue Jays and immediately had a significant impact on the team. A mere two seasons later, he helped the Jays win back-to-back World Series titles. Today, Roberto is considered one of the best clutch hitters in the American League and his popularity continues to boost Blue Jay attendance.

**So You Want to Know—**
How Mr. and Mrs. Alomar keep track of their sons? Roberto's mother and father bought a satellite dish and put it on the roof of their house in Salinas, California, so that they can watch Roberto and brother Sandy play, wherever they are!

## Vital Stats

➤ Height: 6'0"
➤ Weight: 185
➤ Birthplace: Ponce, Puerto Rico
➤ Current residence: Toronto, Ontario
➤ Nickname: Robby
➤ Hobbies: playing miniature golf; listening to music, especially Paula Abdul; driving speedboats

## Cool Credits

➤ Tied American League single-season record for fewest errors by a second baseman (five), 1992
➤ Won American League Golden Glove at second base, 1991–1994

## Birthday Beat

*February 5, 1968*

Roberto Alomar
c/o The Toronto Blue Jays
The Toronto Skydome
1 Blue Jays Way
Toronto, Ontario
Canada M5V 1J1

# Charles Barkley

▼▼▼▼▼▼▼▼▼▼▼▼▼▼▼▼▼▼▼▼▼

*I*n the NBA there are a lot of great players, but only a few who've been recognized as superstars. Charles Barkley is one of them. He's a player who can take over the game. He's one of the greatest rebounders of all time, one who consistently can snatch a rebound and dribble the length of the court for a one man coast-to-coast fast-break dunk. He can shoot three pointers. He can post up against players much taller than himself. He's built like a football player with the agility of a ballet dancer. And, he's a team leader who took the Phoenix Suns from being simply a good team to being perennial championship contenders.

## Birthday Beat
*February 20, 1963*

**18**

## Cool Credits

➤ NCAA Southeast Conference Player of the Year, 1983
➤ NBA all-rookie team, 1985
➤ All-star team every year since 1986
➤ All-NBA first team, 1988–1991, 1993
➤ Olympic gold medal, 1992
➤ NBA Most Valuable Player, 1993
➤ Shares single-game playoff record for most free throws made in one half (nineteen) and most field goals made in one half (fifteen)

## Vital Stats

➤ Height: 6'6"
➤ Weight: 250
➤ Birthplace: Leeds, Alabama
➤ College: Auburn
➤ Current residence: Phoenix, Arizona
➤ Nicknames: The Round Mound of Rebound, Sir Charles
➤ In his spare time: plays a lot of golf

Charles Barkley
c/o The Phoenix Suns
America West Arena
201 E. Jefferson
Phoenix, AZ 85004

# Bonnie Blair

## Cool Credits

Olympic gold medal in the 500 meters, 1988, 1992, 1994
➤ Olympic gold medal in the 1,000 meters, 1992, 1994
➤ Only American woman ever to win gold in three consecutive Olympics, 1988, 1992, 1994
➤ Only woman in the world to win the 500-meter speed-skating event three Olympics in a row, 1988, 1992, 1994
➤ *Sports Illustrated* Sportswoman of the Year, 1994

## Vital Stats

➤ Height: 5'5"
➤ Weight: 130

➤ Birthplace: Cornwall, New York
➤ Current residence: Milwaukee, Wisconsin
➤ Favorite athlete: Michael Jordan
➤ In her spare time: plays golf, reads, bakes cookies
➤ Favorite car: Jeep Cherokee
➤ Biggest thrill: winning her first Olympic gold medal at Calgary, Alberta, Canada, 1988

*B*onnie Blair is the most decorated woman in U.S. Olympic history, with five gold medals and the potential to win more. She already holds the record as the all-time winningest U.S. winter Olympian with a total of six medals, and she has the chance to break even more records at the 1998 Olympics to be held in Nagano, Japan.

## Birthday Beat
*March 18, 1964*

**So You Want to Know—**
What Bonnie's coach, Nick Thometz, has to say about the Olympic champ? He says, "You can talk all day about her accomplishments, but two things impress me most about Bonnie. One is her longevity . . . Secondly, and I'm around her all the time, she's the same person that she was before her success."

Bonnie Blair
c/o Advantage International, Inc.
1751 Pinnacle Dr., Suite 1500
McLean, VA 22102

# Barry Bonds

onsidered by many to be the best and most exciting player in all of baseball today, right fielder Barry Bonds continues to get better and better. His teammates know that when the game is on the line and Barry Bonds is at the plate, chances are good he will come through with the heroic hit to score the runs and pull out a victory. In fact, Barry bats so well under pressure that many pitchers will walk him intentionally instead of giving him the chance to swing the bat and drive in a game-winning run!

## Cool Credits

➤ National League Most Valuable Player, 1990, 1992, 1993
➤ National League all-star team, 1990, 1992–1994
➤ Led the National League in intentional walks in 1992–1994
➤ National League home run champion, 1993

**So You Want to Know—**

Why Barry has chosen to wear the numbers he's had? When Barry was with the Pittsburgh Pirates, he wore number twenty-four to honor his godfather, Willie Mays. Barry's number with the San Francisco Giants is twenty-five—the number once worn by his dad, Bobby Bonds, now a first-base coach with the Giants.

## Vital Stats

➤ Height: 6'1"
➤ Weight: 195
➤ Birthplace: Riverside, California
➤ College: Arizona State University
➤ Current residence: Murietta, California
➤ Nickname: Barry U.S. Bonds

➤ In his spare time: plays golf with his dad, former big leaguer Bobby Bonds
➤ Career goal: "To walk away from baseball (when I retire), knowing I've left nothing undone."
➤ Idol growing up: his godfather, Willie Mays

## Birthday Beat
*July 24, 1964*

Barry Bonds
c/o The San Francisco Giants
Candlestick Park
San Francisco, CA 94124

# Joe Carter

▼▼▼▼▼▼▼▼▼▼▼▼▼▼▼▼▼▼▼▼

*I*n game six of the 1993 World Series, Joe Carter hit one of the most dramatic home runs in championship history: a game-winning, ninth-inning blast that traveled about 450 feet and gave the Toronto Blue Jays their second straight World Series title. In eleven major league seasons, Joe has averaged twenty-five home runs and ninety RBIs (runs batted in) each season. Some seasons have been more prosperous than others, such as in 1989, when Joe hit thirty-five home runs, and in 1986 and 1993, when he hit 121 RBIs. He is the picture of consistency and his continual ball slugging has catapulted the Blue Jays to many winning seasons.

## Cool Credits

➤ Sporting News College Player of the Year, 1981
➤ American League all-star team, 1991–1994
➤ Holds American League record for most games with three or more home runs (five)

## Vital Stats

➤ Height: 6'3"
➤ Weight: 225
➤ Birthplace: Oklahoma City, Oklahoma
➤ College: Wichita State
➤ Current residence: Toronto, Ontario

## Birthday Beat

*March 7, 1960*

## So You Want to Know—

How difficult it is to hit three home runs in a single game? A three-home-run performance is even more rare than a no-hitter, and Joe has done it five times (and counting) in his illustrious career. He has slugged balls out of the park against the toughest pitchers as well as against relief pitchers whose sole purpose is to enter a game and shut down all home-run production.

Joe Carter
c/o The Toronto Blue Jays
The Toronto Skydome
1 Blue Jays Way, Suite 3200
Toronto, Ontario
Canada M5V 1J1

# Michael Chang

**M**ichael Chang has been a nationally ranked tennis player since he was just seven years old! He's been a pro since he was sixteen and won his first tournament at the age of seventeen. But Michael is more than just a tennis prodigy. He can return the hardest serves and is one of the smartest tennis players around. You can almost see the wheels in his head turning as he strategizes his next shot. He plays tennis like a game of chess, always thinking ahead to his next move.

**Birthday Beat**
*February 22, 1972*

## Vital Stats

➤ Height: 5'9"
➤ Weight: 150
➤ Birthplace: Hoboken, New Jersey
➤ Current residence: Henderson, Nevada
➤ Nickname: Grasshopper (because he bounces around a lot on the court)
➤ In his spare time: likes to go deep-sea fishing, breeds tropical fish
➤ Favorite food: Chinese dumplings, tofu
➤ Idols growing up: tennis stars Jimmy Connors and Bjorn Borg

## Cool Credits

➤ Youngest player (fifteen years old) to win a main draw match in U.S. Open history
➤ French Open winner, 1989
➤ Youngest player to ever rank in the Top 5, August 7, 1989
➤ Won three titles and rose to a career-best number-four ranking, 1992
➤ Top 10 ranking, 1992, 1993, 1994

### So You Want to Know—

How Michael stays in great shape? He watches his diet very carefully by loading up on fruit, steamed vegetables, and rice. He also snacks on a powdered phosphate drink called Stim-o-Stam, which helps prevent muscle cramping.

Michael Chang
c/o Advantage International, Inc.
1751 Pinnacle Dr., Suite 1500
McLean, VA 22102

# Laura Davies

□ □ □ □ □ □ □ □ □ □ □ □ □ □ □ □ □ □ □

*L*aura Davies is one of the hottest players in women's golf and also one whose passion extends beyond the sporting world. Laura not only collects golfing championships and awards, but she also collects televisions and teddy bears. She owns twelve television sets and one hundred teddy bears!

Regarding her golf game, while Laura sometimes has a hard time getting the ball from the fairway onto the green, she is a natural at sinking the ball in the cup once it's on the green. And her many tournament championships prove it!

## Vital Stats

➤ Birthplace: Coventry, England
➤ Current residence: West Byfleet, England
➤ Joined the LPGA: 1987
➤ Low career round: sixty-two
➤ LPGA career holes-in-one: one
➤ Longest measured drive: 351 yards, in Hawaii, 1988

➤ Favorite restaurant: McDonalds
➤ Favorite sports: darts, snooker (a form of billiards), Ping-Pong, basketball, tennis, and swimming
➤ Major influence: professional golfer David Regan

## Birthday Beat

*October 5, 1963*

## So You Want to Know—

How many tournaments Laura won in 1994? Eight! This is very impressive considering that some golfers don't even play eight tournaments in a year. Laura won three in the United States, two in Europe, and one each in Thailand, Japan, and Australia. She said she could have won five more if she had sunk her fair share of putts. "When you don't putt well, you don't win."

## Cool Credits

➤ U.S. Women's Open Winner, 1987
➤ Named a Member of the British Empire (M.B.E.) by Queen Elizabeth II (one of the highest honors in Britain), 1988
➤ Won the Standard Register Ping, the Sara Lee Classic, and the LPGA Championship, 1994

Laura Davies
c/o LPGA Headquarters
2750 W. International Speedway Blvd.,
Suite B
Daytona Beach, FL 32114

# Patrick Ewing

▼▼▼▼▼▼▼▼▼▼▼▼▼▼▼▼▼▼▼▼▼

**P**atrick Ewing didn't start playing ball until he was thirteen, when he moved with his family from Kingston, Jamaica, to Massachusetts. He wasn't very good at first, but he decided that he wanted to be a great basketball player one day. From then on, he excelled every step of the way. Today Patrick is a perennial all-star player and is considered one of the most versatile centers in the NBA. He has led the New York Knicks deep into the play-offs for several years and into the NBA finals in 1994. Before retiring, he wants the ultimate team victory, a championship ring for him and all his teammates!

**Birthday Beat**
*August 5, 1962*

## Cool Credits

➤ Olympic gold medal, 1984, 1992
➤ NCAA championship with Georgetown, 1984
➤ NCAA Player of the Year, 1985
➤ Drafted number one overall in NBA draft, 1985
➤ NBA Rookie of the Year, 1986
➤ All-NBA first team, 1990
➤ Holds NBA Finals single-series record for most blocked shots (thirty), 1994

## Vital Stats

➤ Height: 7'0"
➤ Weight: 240
➤ Birthplace: Kingston, Jamaica
➤ College: Georgetown University

➤ Current residence: Fort Lee, New Jersey
➤ Full name: Patrick Aloysius Ewing
➤ In his spare time: listens to reggae music and the blues, watches boxing and football
➤ Favorite food: curried goat and other Jamaican specialties

### So You Want to Know—

When Patrick Ewing wound up on the same team as Michael Jordan? It happened in the 1984 Olympics. Ewing and Jordan were the team's star players. They won the gold medal and no team even came close to beating them!

Patrick Ewing
c/o The New York Knickerbockers
Madison Square Garden
2 Penn Plaza
New York, NY 10121

# Mary Joe Fernandez

■ ■ ■ ■ ■ ■ ■ ■ ■ ■ ■ ■ ■ ■ ■

*M*ary Joe Fernandez is one of the most promising young players on the professional tennis tour. While her career started late due, in part, to her desire to complete her education first, her star is quickly on the rise. Mary Joe is known for playing a cautious game, hanging back at the baseline. Recently, though, she has become more aggressive, charging the net with regularity. As she continues to play and improve, Mary Joe may find her place among the tennis elite and achieve a number-one ranking before long.

## Cool Credits

➤ Youngest player ever to win a U.S. Open match (at fourteen)
➤ Top 10 ranking, 1990–1993
➤ Ranked number four in the world (becoming first highest-ranked American other than Chris Evert or Martina Navratilova since 1980), 1990
➤ Olympic gold medal in doubles (with Gigi Fernandez), 1992
➤ Olympic bronze medal in singles, 1992

## Vital Stats

➤ Height: 5'10"
➤ Weight: 140
➤ Birthplace: Dominican Republic
➤ Current residence: Miami, Florida
➤ Nickname: May Jay
➤ Turned pro: 1986

## So You Want to Know—

What education means to Mary Joe? It meant enough for her to postpone joining the pro tennis tour. Many tennis stars either drop out of high school or finish high school using private tutors, but Mary Joe stayed at Carrollton School of the Sacred Heart in Miami until she was able to wear a cap and gown and accept her diploma with her classmates.

➤ In her spare time: hangs out with her friends, plays golf, goes waterskiing and wave running
➤ Favorite food: Cuban
➤ Childhood idol: tennis star Chris Evert

## Birthday Beat

*August 19, 1971*

Mary Joe Fernandez
c/o Women's Tennis Association
World Headquarters
133 First Street N.E.
St. Petersburg, FL 33701

# Steffi Graf

## Cool Credits

➤ Designed own line of tennis apparel for Adidas
➤ Olympic gold medal, 1988
➤ Olympic silver medal, 1992
➤ Winner of fifteen Grand Slam singles titles
➤ Top 10 ranking, 1985–1994
➤ Ranked number one, 1987–1990, 1993, 1994

## Vital Stats

➤ Height: 5'9"
➤ Weight: 132
➤ Birthplace: Mannheim, Germany
➤ Current residence: Bruhl, Germany, and Del Rey Beach, Florida
➤ In her spare time: enjoys reading (especially Stephen King novels), playing cards, collecting T-shirts, listening to Bruce Springsteen and Phil Collins
➤ Pets: two German shepherds, Max and Zar, and a boxer named Ben
➤ Favorite food: barilla pasta

## Birthday Beat

*June 14, 1969*

34

☐ ☐ ☐ ☐ ☐ ☐ ☐ ☐ ☐ ☐ ☐ ☐ ☐ ☐ ☐ ☐ ☐ ☐

*S*teffi Graf is one of the best (if not the best) female tennis players in the world. Her serve can be devastating, and her size, strength, and speed make her a force to be reckoned with at the net. Steffi is also very consistent—once winning sixty-six games in a row (between 1989 and 1990). Steffi is one of only five players ever to win the Grand Slam—victories at the Australian Open, the French Open, Wimbledon, and the U.S. Open, all in the same year. So what's left to accomplish? Steffi's ultimate goal is perhaps the hardest of all for someone with the immense pressures of a professional tennis player: to enjoy playing.

### So You Want to Know—

One of Steffi's most amazing tennis achievements? She maintained a number-one ranking for 186 weeks (between 1987 and 1990), the longest reign of any tennis player, male or female!

Steffi Graf
c/o Advantage International, Inc.
1751 Pinnacle Dr., Suite 1500
McLean, VA 22102

**35**

# Ken Griffey, Jr.

▼▼▼▼▼▼▼▼▼▼▼▼▼▼▼▼▼▼▼▼

*W*hen Ken Griffey, Jr., was a kid, he had the kind of privileges most youngsters don't have. His father played for the "Big Red Machine"—the Cincinnati Reds of the '70s—and he was able to visit his dad in the clubhouse at Riverfront Stadium in Cincinnati. "Junior" knew all the great Reds players like Pete Rose, Johnny Bench, and Tony Perez.

Today Ken plays for the Seattle Mariners and has seemed to have mastered every aspect of the game—hitting, base running, and fielding. He has a great chance of winning the Triple Crown (achieving the highest batting average, the most home runs, and the most RBIs in his league in one season) at least once before his career is over.

## Cool Credits

➤ Ken Griffey, Sr., and Ken Griffey, Jr., became the first father and son to play on the same big league team in the same season, 1990

➤ American League all-star team, 1990–1995
➤ All-star Most Valuable Player, 1992
➤ Shares major league record for most consecutive games with one or more home runs (eight), 1993

## Vital Stats

➤ Height: 6'3"
➤ Weight: 205
➤ Birthplace: Donora, Pennsylvania
➤ Current residence: Seattle, Washington
➤ Nickname: Junior, The Natural
➤ Favorite athlete: Deion Sanders
➤ Idol growing up: Rickey Henderson

## Birthday Beat

*November 21, 1969*

## So You Want to Know—

Why Ken chose to wear the number twenty-four? Some people think he chose it because it was the number worn by his hero, legendary Giants star Willie Mays. Actually, Ken likes the number twenty-four because that is the most home runs that he ever hit in a single season—and the only time he ever hit more home runs than his father. He did it during his senior year at Moeller High School in Cincinnati.

Ken Griffey, Jr.
c/o The Seattle Mariners
P.O. Box 4100
Seattle, WA 98104

# Tony Gwynn

*I*f there is a hitting "scientist" in baseball, it's Tony Gwynn. He studies the art of hitting the way Red Sox Hall-of-Famer Ted Williams did. He is a perennial National League all-star player and has spent his entire fourteen-year career with the San Diego Padres. His batting average was .394 in 1994, and if the strike had not shortened the season, Tony could quite possibly have hit .400, a feat that hasn't been accomplished in over fifty years!

## So You Want to Know —

How Tony Gywnn rates against the best hitters of all time? Five times in his career, Tony has gotten five hits in one game. In this century, only three players have had more than five hits in a game, Ty Cobb (fourteen), Pete Rose (ten), and Max Carey (nine).

## Cool Credits

➤ National League Batting Champion, 1984, 1987, 1989, 1994

## Birthday Beat

*May 9, 1960*

➤ Highest batting average in National League (.394) since Stan Musial hit .376 in 1948, 1994
➤ Golden Glove Award (best oufielder in National League), 1986, 1987, 1989–1991
➤ National League all-star Team, 1984–1994

## Vital Stats

➤ Height: 5'11"
➤ Weight: 215
➤ Birthplace: Los Angeles, California
➤ College: San Diego State University
➤ Current residence: San Diego, California
➤ In his spare time: plays basketball

Tony Gywnn
c/o The San Diego Padres
Jack Murphy Stadium
9449 Friars Rd.
San Diego, CA 92108

# Anfernee Hardaway

□ □ □ □ □ □ □ □ □ □ □ □ □ □ □ □

*A*nfernee Hardaway came into his own in only his second season in the NBA. Many sportswriters consider him a bona fide superstar and a team leader reminiscent of Magic Johnson. With keen court vision and spectacular passing, Orlando's all-star point guard is a one-man gang. Anfernee leaves both fans and foes breathless with his skillful bounce and no-look passes. Together with his Orlando Magic teammates, especially Shaquille O'Neal, Anfernee seems destined to win an NBA championship.

### So You Want to Know—

How Anfernee spent the money from his big rookie contract? He bought his grandmother a comfortable red-brick home with white pillars on four acres in East Memphis. The big-time hoopster says there's so much land around his grandmother's home, he's going to build a huge park for all of his little cousins and nieces and nephews. "It will be a place where children can go for a little luxury and a lot of love."

## Vital Stats

➤ Height: 6'7"
➤ Weight: 200
➤ Birthplace: Memphis, Tennessee
➤ College: Memphis State (now University of Memphis)
➤ Current residence: Orlando, Florida
➤ Nickname: Penny
➤ Idol growing up: his grandmother Louise

## Cool Credits

➤ NCAA all-American first team, 1993
➤ NBA all-rookie first team, 1994

## Birthday Beat

*July 18, 1972*

Anfernee Hardaway
c/o International Management Group
22 E. 71st St.
New York, NY 10021

# Brett Hull

*T*he name *Hull* was known in the world of professional hockey even before Brett Hull started playing. His father, Bobby Hull, is a living hockey legend who played for many illustrious seasons with the Chicago Black Hawks. He was known as the "Golden Jet" because he skated like the wind. But recently, Brett has become just as golden and possibly better known than his dad. Brett is a hard-nosed player who worked his way up the ranks with a vicious slap shot that has been timed at ninety miles per hour. Brett works relentlessly to make the St. Louis Blues a strong contender for the Stanley Cup every season.

### So You Want to Know—

How Brett compares to his father, Bobby Hull? Brett and Bobby are the first father and son in pro hockey history to each score fifty or more goals in a season. Hull and Hull, who have 966 goals between them, should overtake Gordie and Mark Howe—who together have a career total of 1,009 goals—to become the highest scoring father/son combination ever.

## Cool Credits

➤ Led the league in goals (seventy-two), power-play goals (twenty-seven), game-winning goals (twelve), and hat tricks (five), 1989–1990
➤ Lady Byng Trophy (The Most Gentlemanly Player), 1990
➤ Hart Trophy (NHL Most Valuable Player), 1991
➤ Shares NHL record with Wayne Gretzky as one of only two players to score seventy goals or more in three different seasons

## Vital Stats

➤ Height: 5'10"
➤ Weight: 203

➤ Birthplace: Belleville, Ontario, Canada
➤ Current residence: Duluth, Minnesota
➤ Nickname: The Incredible Hull, The Golden Brett
➤ In his spare time: plays golf
➤ Idols growing up: golfer Jack Nicklaus, rocker Mick Jagger
➤ Favorite cat: his cat, Layla

## Birthday Beat

*August 9, 1964*

Brett Hull
c/o The St. Louis Blues
1401 Clark Ave.
St. Louis, MO 63103

# Michael Irvin

■ ■ ■ ■ ■ ■ ■ ■ ■ ■ ■ ■ ■ ■ ■ ■ ▪ ▪ ▪ ▪ ▪ ▪

*O*ne of the best receivers in pro football, Michael Irvin is the perfect counterpart to Dallas Cowboy's quarterback Troy Aikman. As one of seventeen kids, Michael might have gotten lost in the crowd as a kid, but he doesn't have much trouble being noticed these days. He's famous for his spectacular catches, and in only seven seasons he's broken most Cowboy receiving records and has been to the Pro Bowl four times. The secret to his success? "When I step onto the field," he says, "I have the attitude that I'm the best on that field."

## Cool Credits

➤ NCAA all-American at Miami University, where he caught the game-winning touchdown pass that beat Oklahoma State in the Orange Bowl, 1988
➤ Became the first rookie to start as wide receiver for the Cowboys since Bob Hayes in 1965, 1988
➤ Led the NFC with a 20.4 yards-per-catch average, 1988
➤ Pro Bowl team, 1991–1994

## Vital Stats

➤ Height: 6'2"
➤ Weight: 205
➤ Birthplace: Fort Lauderdale, Florida
➤ High school: St. Thomas Aquinas, Fort Lauderdale
➤ College: Miami

44

➤ Current residence: Carrollton, Texas
➤ Nickname: The Playmaker
➤ In his spare time: plays basketball, spends time with his large family

## So You Want to Know—

How charitable Michael is? In each of the past three training camps, he has teamed up with Southwest Airlines to fly nearly one hundred underprivileged children to Dallas to spend the day with the Cowboys.

## Birthday Beat
*March 5, 1966*

Michael Irvin
c/o Steve Endicott
15303 Dallas Parkway, Suite 970
Dallas, TX 75248

# Larry Johnson

❑ ❑ ❑ ❑ ❑ ❑ ❑ ❑ ❑ ❑ ❑

## Vital Stats

➤ Height: 6'7"
➤ Weight: 250
➤ Birthplace:
Tyler, Texas
➤ College:
University of
Nevada, Las
Vegas
➤ Current
residences:
Dallas, Texas and
Lake Wylie, North
Carolina
➤ Nickname:
Grandmama
➤ Full name: Larry
Demetric Johnson
➤ In his spare time: likes
to visit his old
neighborhood in
southern Dallas, go to
the movies, and listen
to music

## Birthday Beat

*March 14, 1969*

## Cool Credits

➤ Junior College Player
of the Year (Odessa
Junior College), 1988,
1989
➤ NCAA Player of the
Year, 1991
➤ Number-one draft pick
(drafted by the Charlotte
Hornets), 1991
➤ NBA Rookie of the
Year, 1992
➤ All-star team, 1993,
1994

46

*A*fter only four seasons in the NBA, Larry Johnson has established himself as a superstar. He can do it all: shoot, rebound, handle the ball, and play tough defense. He has speed, quickness, and great strength. He's a great scorer as well as an unselfish passer. More than anything, though, the confidence he's carried with him since he was a high school freshman starting on the varsity team is sure to take him to countless more victories.

### So You Want to Know—

About Larry's nickname? He is featured in famous sneaker commercials where he plays the part of his own grandmother slam dunking a basketball. The ads are so popular that Larry keeps making them. "Grandmama goes up and slams so hard I keep waiting for her to come down with the rim in her hand," says Larry.

Larry Johnson
c/o The Charlotte Hornets
100 Hive Dr.
Charlotte, NC 28217

# Michael Jordan

▼▼▼▼▼▼▼▼▼▼▼▼▼▼▼▼▼▼

*A*rguably the greatest basketball player ever, Michael Jordan retired from the NBA in 1993 to try his hand at baseball. He signed a minor league contract with the Chicago White Sox and played a season in the Arizona Winter League for the Flagstaff Scorpions. He also played one season with the Birmingham (Alabama) Barons, the White Sox's AAA affiliate.

But now, he's back on the hardwood. When he eventually retires—and stays retired—he'll leave behind the most sensational legacy in NBA history.

### So You Want to Know—

How much fans will pay to see Michael Jordan play? Some fans in New York paid as much as $1000 per ticket to see Michael play against the New York Knicks on March 28, 1995, in his first game since his 1993 retirement.

## Cool Credits

➤ NCAA Championship with the University of North Carolina, 1982
➤ Drafted third overall in the NBA draft, 1984
➤ Olympic gold medals, 1984, 1992
➤ NBA Rookie of the Year, 1985
➤ All-star team, 1985, 1987–1993
➤ NBA Most Valuable Player, 1988, 1991–1993
➤ NBA all-defensive team, 1987–1993
➤ NBA Championship, 1991–1993

## Vital Stats

➤ Height: 6'6"
➤ Weight: 198
➤ Birthplace: Brooklyn, New York
➤ College: University of North Carolina
➤ Current residence: Chicago, Illinois
➤ Nickname: His Airness, Air Jordan
➤ In his spare time: plays golf and billiards, bowls, watches stock car races
➤ Idol growing up: his father

## Birthday Beat

*February 17, 1963*

• • • • • • • • • • • • • • • • • • • • • • • • • • • • • • •

Michael Jordan
c/o Barbara Allen
FAME
5335 Wisconsin Ave. NW, Suite 850
Washington D.C. 20015

*or try:*
Air Jordan Flight Club
One Bowerman Drive
Beaverton, OR 97005

# David Justice

■ ■ ■ ■ ■ ■ ■ ■ ■ ■ ■ ■ ■ ■

*I*n the late 1980s the Atlanta Braves were labeled "America's Team" by a loyal Atlanta TV station, despite having one mediocre season after another. In 1989, the Braves brought up a bright and talented outfielder named David Justice from their minor league team in Richmond, Virginia. In his next season, his first full season, Dave won the National League Rookie of the Year award. At first, he allowed this success to go to his head. He reported to spring training the next season dripping with gold jewelry. He even refused to sign autographs for his fans. Since then, Dave has regained his humility and his appreciation for his fans. He's become an all-star player and is one of the primary reasons the Braves have been so successful in the 1990s.

## Cool Credits

➤ National League Rookie of the Year, 1990
➤ Holds major league single-season record for fewest errors by out-fielder who once led the league in errors (eight), 1992
➤ Named outfielder on The Sporting News National League Silver Slugger team, 1993

## Birthday Beat
*April 14, 1966*

### So You Want to Know—
Who the love of David's life is? He's married to famous actress Halle Berry. Just like Yankee outfielder Joe DiMaggio, who was married to movie star Marilyn Monroe, David and Halle make headlines whenever they go out together in public.

### Vital Stats
➤ Height: 6'3"
➤ Weight: 200
➤ Birthplace: Cincinnati, Ohio
➤ College: Thomas More College (Crestview, Kentucky)
➤ Current residence: Atlanta, Georgia

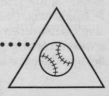

David Justice
c/o The Atlanta Braves
P.O. Box 4064
Atlanta, GA 30302

# Michelle Kwan

ichelle Kwan was selected to the 1994 U.S. Olympic figure skating team as an alternate when Nancy Kerrigan was injured in an attack. Although Nancy's recovery kept Michelle from competing in Lillehammer, Norway, Michelle is considered to be one of the most promising newcomers in the world of figure skating.

She started skating at age five and won her first competition at only seven years old. When Michelle watched champion skater Brian Boitano perform his difficult routine in the 1988 Winter Olympics, she decided to also strive to win an Olympic gold medal. Because one of Michelle's greatest assets is her driving ambition, this goal is clearly in her sight.

## Cool Credits

➤ Youngest skating champion to ever win four major events at the U.S. Olympic Festival, 1993
➤ Landed six triple jumps at the U.S. Olympic Festival, 1993
➤ Placed second in two significant events at the Goodwill Games and the Pro-Am Championships, 1994
➤ Won the International Challenge, 1995

## Vital Stats

➤ Current residence: Torrance, California
➤ Nickname: Little Kwan
➤ In her spare time: swims, does her homework
➤ Languages: besides English, speaks Chinese and French

➤ Favorite athlete: Michael Jordan
➤ Favorite pets: cats and cockatiels
➤ Favorite movie: *In the Line of Fire*

## Birthday Beat

*July 7, 1980*

### So You Want to Know—

The significance of the necklace you've seen around Michelle's neck? The necklace she always wears—on and off the rink—was a very special gift from her grandmother, given to Michelle's parents when she was born. It's a Chinese good luck charm.

Michelle Kwan
c/o Proper Marketing Associates
322 Vista Del Mar
Redondo Beach, CA 90277

# Mario Lemieux

**N**obody has ever questioned Mario Lemieux's talent. He's been compared to the greatest hockey players of all time: Wayne Gretzky, Bobby Orr, and Gordie Howe. Today he is also thought of as one of the most courageous competitors in any sport.

In 1992, Mario was diagnosed with a form of cancer called Hodgkin's disease. He had surgery to remove the cancer cells from his neck and continued his treatment by receiving radiation. Despite this serious condition, Mario has refused to allow his illness to sideline him for long. Just twelve hours after his last radiation treatment, Mario hit the ice, scoring a goal and adding an assist!

## Vital Stats
➤ Height: 6'4"
➤ Weight: 210
➤ Birthplace: Montreal, Quebec, Canada
➤ Current residence: Pittsburgh, Pennsylvania

➤ Name: in French, Lemieux translates into "the best"
➤ In his spare time: plays golf and video games

## Birthday Beat
*October 5, 1965*

## Cool Credits

➤ Scored a goal the very first shot he ever took in the NHL, 1985
➤ Calder Memorial Trophy (best rookie in NHL), 1985
➤ NHL scoring champion, 1988, 1989, 1992
➤ Hart Trophy (NHL Most Valuable Player), 1988
➤ Corn Smith Trophy (Most Valuable Player in playoffs), 1991, 1992
➤ Back-to-back Stanley Cup Championships with Pittsburgh Penguins, 1991, 1992
➤ Ross Trophy (NHL leading scorer), 1988, 1989, 1992, 1993

## So You Want to Know—

Who Mario's greatest inspiration has been? His biggest inspiration is also his greatest competitor: Wayne Gretzky. When Mario entered the NHL, he was a little overconfident about his abilities. Then he played in the first Canada Cup—on the same team as Gretzky.

Mario Lemieux
c/o The Pittsburgh Penguins
Civic Arena, Gate 9
Pittsburgh, PA 15219

# Eric Lindros

■ ■ ■ ■ ■ ■ ■ ■ ■ ■ ■ ■ ■ ■ ■ ■ ■

*A*t sixteen, Eric Lindros was so much bigger and more gifted than the other teens in his hockey league that coaches in Ontario began comparing him to some of the greatest players of all time! In the 1990–1991 season, in only fifty-seven games he scored 149 points for his minor league team, the Oshawa Generals, and won several Junior Hockey League awards.

His talent has continued to blossom. He contributed mightily to Canada's silver medal victory at the Albertville Olympics in 1992. Now with the Philadelphia Flyers, Eric combines phenomenal speed, strength, scoring, skating, and puck-handling ability. He won't back down from any challenge.

## Cool Credits

➤ Drafted first overall by the Quebec Nordiques in the NHL Entry Draft, 1991
➤ Traded from Quebec to the Philadelphia Flyers for six players, two draft picks, and $15 million, 1992
➤ Olympic silver medal, 1992
➤ Recorded seven career hat tricks (scoring three or more goals in a game), as of 1995
➤ Bobby Clarke Trophy winner (the Flyer's Most Valuable Player), 1995

## Birthday Beat

*February 28, 1973*

### So You Want to Know—

What Eric does to give something back to the Philadelphia community? He participates in a number of charitable and community activities during the off-season, including a Philadelphia-area youth hockey school and a charity golf tournament.

## Vital Stats

➤ Height: 6'4"
➤ Weight: 235
➤ Birthplace: London, Ontario, Canada
➤ Current residence: Toronto, Ontario
➤ In his spare time: likes to waterski, play golf, and listen to music (especially Bryan Adams and Asia)

Eric Lindros
c/o The Philadelphia Flyers
Core States Spectrum
3601 S. Broad St.
Philadelphia, PA 19148

# Rebecca Lobo

*R*ebecca Lobo may not exactly be a household name, but ever since her basketball team, the University of Connecticut Lady Huskies, won the NCAA National Championship in the 1994–1995 season, she has made headlines all over the country. Rebecca led the nation's top-ranked Huskies to a perfect 34–0 season, a remarkable achievement to say the least, especially considering it's only the second time in history a women's team has gone undefeated.

Rebecca first made believers out of an entire campus, and then out of an entire nation as the country watched UConn beat Tennessee in a hard-fought battle aired over national television. Rebecca credits her determination to her parents, who, she says, "never let their kids walk away from something because it was too hard."

**Birthday Beat**
*October 6, 1973*

## Cool Credits

➤ All-time leading scorer, male or female, in Massachusetts state high school history (2,710 points)
➤ NCAA Championship with UConn, 1995
➤ Academic all-American first team at UConn, 1995

## Vital Stats

➤ Height: 6'4"
➤ Weight: 180
➤ Hometown: Southwick, Massachusetts
➤ College: University of Connecticut
➤ Nickname: LoboCop
➤ Idol growing up: David Robinson

### So You Want to Know—

Which basketball team was Rebecca's favorite when she was young? Growing up in Massachusetts, she rooted for the Boston Celtics. In fourth grade, Rebecca wrote a fan letter to the president of the Celtics, Red Auerbach. The letter said, "I'm a really big fan. I want you to know I'm going to be the first girl to play for the Celtics."

Rebecca Lobo
c/o Director of Athletics
The University of Connecticut
2095 Hillside Rd. U-78
Storrs, CT 06269-3078
*(Although Rebecca recently graduated, the UConn Athletic Department still looks after her fan mail.)*

# Dan Marino

## Cool Credits

➤ Drafted in the first round, twenty-seventh overall, by the Miami Dolphins, 1983
➤ AFL Player of the Year, 1984
➤ Quarterback for the Dolphins in Super Bowl XIX, 1984
➤ Quarterback for the Dolphins in the AFC Championship game, 1984, 1985, 1992, 1994
➤ AFC's top-rated passer (89.2) and the AFC leader in touchdown passes (thirty), 1994

## Vital Stats

➤ Height: 6'4"
➤ Weight: 224
➤ Birthplace: Pittsburgh, Pennsylvania
➤ Full name: Daniel Constantine Marino, Jr.
➤ High school: Central Catholic (Pittsburgh)
➤ College: University of Pittsburgh

➤ Current residence: Miami, Florida
➤ Brother-in-law: Bill Maas, nose tackle for the Kansas City Chiefs and Green Bay Packers, 1984–1993

### So You Want to Know—

How Dan keeps busy during the off-season? Dan makes commercials and other TV appearances when he is not on the football field. Every Christmas season you can see his Isotoner glove commercials on TV. He also represents Frito-Lay, among other companies. But he probably had the best time acting when he played himself in the movie *Ace Ventura, Pet Detective* with Jim Carrey.

**D**an Marino has been a quarterback since junior high school and a Miami Dolphin since being drafted into the NFL in 1983. Although Dan was also drafted by the Kansas City Royals, he chose to concentrate on just one sport. It seems he made the right choice because he's now one of the greatest quarterbacks of all time! Year after year he is rated one of the top passers in football, and consequently, the Dolphins are always a competitive offensive machine. Dan often saves his best passes for the fourth quarter, which makes the games he plays the most exciting to watch.

## Birthday Beat
*September 15, 1961*

Dan Marino
c/o Dan Marino Foundation
1063 Shotgun Rd.
Sunrise, FL 33326

# Reggie Miller

*T*o say athletic ability runs in Reggie Miller's family is an understatement. His brother Darrell played baseball with the California Angels from 1984 to 1988, and his sister Cheryl, a UCLA alumna, is regarded as the best female college basketball player ever. Reggie was also a collegiate star for the UCLA Bruins and a top draft pick. He went on to be a solid offensive player his first few seasons in the NBA with the Indiana Pacers, and in the 1994 playoffs, he almost single-handedly upset the heavily favored New York Knicks. His most amazing feat to date came during the 1995 playoffs when he scored eight points in eighteen seconds to catapult the Pacers to another exciting comeback victory over the Knickerbockers.

## Cool Credits

➤ Selected by Pacers as a first round draft pick, 1987
➤ Played every game of 1987, 1989–1992 seasons
➤ Holds single-game playoff record for most three-point shots made in one quarter (five), June 1, 1994

## Vital Stats

➤ Height: 6'7"
➤ Weight: 185
➤ Birthplace: Riverside, California
➤ High school: Riverside Polytechnic, Riverside, California
➤ College: University of California, Los Angeles
➤ Current residence: Indianapolis, Indiana

## Birthday Beat

*August 24, 1965*

### So You Want to Know—

How well Reggie played in college? Very well, thank you. Reggie was recruited by the same school his sister Cheryl starred for, UCLA. The Bruins were one of the best teams in the Pac 10 conference with Reggie on their squad. In his last two seasons, he was the team's highest scorer, averaging twenty-three points a game.

Reggie Miller
c/o The Indiana Pacers
Market Square Arena
300 E. Market St.
Indianapolis, IN 46204

# Hakeem Olajuwon

□ □ □ □ □ □ □ □ □ □ □ □ □ □ □ □ □ □

## So You Want to Know—

Why he changed his name from Hakeem to Akeem, and back to Hakeem? When Hakeem emigrated to the United States to play basketball, he dropped the silent "H" so that people would pronounce his name correctly. Once he became a superstar, he changed it back to its original spelling, as he figured that people would make sure to say his name the right way no matter how he spelled it.

## Birthday Beat

*January 21, 1963*

## Cool Credits

➤ Drafted first overall in the NBA draft, 1984
➤ NBA all-rookie team, 1985
➤ NBA Defensive Player of the Year, 1993, 1994
➤ NBA Most Valuable Player, 1994, 1995
➤ NBA Championship, 1994, 1995
➤ Holds career record for highest average blocked shots per game (3.62), 1995

## Vital Stats

➤ Height: 7'0"
➤ Weight: 255
➤ Birthplace: Lagos, Nigeria
➤ High School: Moslem Teachers College (Nigeria)
➤ College: University of Houston
➤ Current residence: Houston, Texas
➤ Nickname: Hakeem the Dream

*H*akeem Olajuwon is the most agile center in the NBA. Watching him move so gracefully on the court, it's easy to forget that he is seven feet tall. Hakeem's athletic skills sometimes seem limitless, and he has accomplished what few athletes in any sport have—championships both in college and in the pros. When he was in college, he led the University of Houston to the Final Four in 1983 and 1984. And his intense work ethic and smart play helped to bring the Houston Rockets an NBA title in 1994.

Hakeem Olajuwon
c/o The Houston Rockets
The Summit
Houston, TX 77046

# Shaquille O'Neal

▼▼▼▼▼▼▼▼▼▼▼▼▼▼▼▼▼▼▼▼▼▼▼

*S*haquille O'Neal is known far and wide as the reigning king of NBA centers. He joined the Orlando Magic as the most publicized rookie with the biggest contract, and he has since continued to live up to the hype. Although he's only played two pro seasons, his scoring prowess and his inside dominance are so impressive, NBA fans are seeing the status of legend in Shaq's future. He has shattered more backboards than any other player since former New Jersey Nets star Daryl "Chocolate Thunder" Dawkins.

## Cool Credits

➤ First team NCAA all-American, 1992
➤ Drafted first overall pick in NBA draft, 1992
➤ All-star team, 1993–1995
➤ NBA Rookie of the Year, 1993
➤ NBA scoring champion, 1995

### So You Want to Know—

What Shaq was doing at Louisiana State University in the summer of 1994? He was working toward his college degree. He was a junior at LSU when he left school to join the NBA in 1992. Shaq promised his mom he would graduate someday and wants to keep his word. "Money is good," Shaq says, "but knowledge is golden."

## Vital Stats

➤ Height: 7'1"
➤ Weight: 301
➤ Birthplace: Newark, New Jersey
➤ College: Louisiana State University
➤ Current residence: Islesworth, Florida
➤ Nickname: Shaq ("Shack"), Shaq-Fu

➤ In his spare time: Shaq likes wild rides. He'd like to have the world's tallest roller coaster and call it Shaq Mountain.
➤ Shoe size: 21EEE (must be custom-made)
➤ License plate: DUNKON-U
➤ Body fat: less than 1%

## Birthday Beat
*March 6, 1972*

Shaquille O'Neal
One-Al Inc.
P.O. Box 951840
Lake Mary, FL 32795-1840

# Mike Piazza

## Vital Stats

➤ Height: 6'3"
➤ Weight: 197
➤ Birthplace: Norristown, Pennsylvania
➤ College: Miami-Dade (North) Community College
➤ Current residence: Los Angeles, California
➤ Favorite food: Italian

## So You Want to Know—

Who in the Piazza family may become Mike's biggest competitor? Actually, Mike's father, Vince Piazza, is a businessman who is trying to buy the San Francisco Giants—arch rivals of Mike's L.A. Dodgers.

■ ■ ■ ■ ■ ■ ■ ■ ■ ■ ■ ■ ■ ■ ■ ■ ■ ■

*I*n 1993, Mike Piazza left the minor league to become the catcher for the Los Angeles Dodgers. Because he is Dodger manager Tommy Lasorda's godson, the press and many fans doubted Mike's true ability. They thought his family connections got him his major league job. Much to everyone's elation, however, Michael Joseph Piazza turned in a rookie season that made Dodger fans proud, winning Rookie of the Year for the National League. This gutsy catcher who was brought up to replace the popular Mike Sciosa quickly earned much respect and many admirers around the league.

## Birthday Beat

*September 4, 1968*

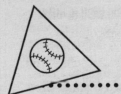

## Cool Credits

➤ National League Rookie of the Year, 1993
➤ Led the National League catchers with ninety-eight assists, 1993
➤ National League all-star team, 1994

Mike Piazza
c/o The Los Angeles Dodgers
1000 Elysian Park Ave.
Los Angeles, CA 90012

# Scottie Pippen

hen the Chicago Bulls traded for an unknown draft pick from a small Arkansas college in 1987, little did sports fans suspect this quiet ballplayer would turn out to be the magnificent Scottie Pippen. The Seattle SuperSonics decided to trade Scottie to the Bulls immediately after drafting him in order to obtain Olden Polynice's draft rights and future draft choices. The Sonics probably wish they had never made the deal. Scottie has blossomed into one of the greatest power forwards in NBA history. With the help of teammate Michael Jordan, Scottie and the Bulls went on a "Bull Run" and captured back-to-back-to-back NBA Championships from 1991–1993.

## Cool Credits

➤ All-star team, 1991–1994
➤ NBA all-defensive first team, 1992–1994
➤ Olympic gold medal, 1992
➤ All-NBA first team, 1994

### So You Want to Know—

Why Scottie is considered the Chicago Bulls' "Iron Man"? For three years in a row, he played all eighty-two games in each season.

□ □ □ □ □ □ □ □ □ □ □ □ □ □ □ □ □ □ □ □ □ □

## Vital Stats

➤ Height: 6'7"
➤ Weight: 225
➤ Birthplace: Hamburg, Arkansas
➤ College: University of Central Arkansas
➤ Current residence: Chicago, Illinois

➤ In his spare time: plays with his son and their dogs, drives powerboats
➤ Idol growing up: Julius Erving ("Dr. J")
➤ Favorite food: steak

## Birthday Beat

*September 25, 1965*

Scottie Pippen
c/o The Chicago Bulls
1 Magnificent Mile
980 N. Michigan Ave., #11600
Chicago, IL 60611-4501

# Gabrielle Reece

▼▼▼▼▼▼▼▼▼▼▼▼▼▼▼▼▼▼▼▼

*A* volleyball game, whether it's professional or amateur, seems to be as much fun for the spectators as it is for the players. And lately, all eyes seem to be on one pro women's beach volleyball player, Gabrielle Reece, with her amazing volleyball skills and physical beauty. In fact, Gabrielle is also becoming one of modeling's top stars. In 1989, when she was only a sophomore at Florida State, *Elle* magazine named her "one of the five most beautiful women in the world." Now, while playing pro volleyball, she plays a supercharged game. She says, "I enjoy getting the ball to go exactly where I want it, at the speed I want it to go."

## Cool Credits

➤ All-metro conference team (Florida State University), 1990
➤ Set Florida State record for total blocks (748), 1990
➤ Set Florida State record for solo blocks (240), 1990

➤ Led Women's Beach Volleyball League (WBVL) in kills (227) and blocks (53), 1993
➤ WBVL Most Valuable Player, 1993
➤ Led WBVL in kills (454), 1994
➤ WBVL Best Offensive Player and Most Improved Player, 1994

## Birthday Beat
*January 6, 1970*

## Vital Stats

➤ Height: 6'3"
➤ College: Florida State University
➤ Current residence: Southern California
➤ Nickname: Gabby
➤ Can be seen on magazine covers: *Elle, Fitness, Shape, Harper's Bazaar, Vogue*
➤ Can be seen on TV: sports correspondent for MTV Sports

### So You Want to Know—

About Gabby's other talents? She is Nike's first-ever female athlete to co-design an athletic shoe. In 1994, Nike launched the Air Trainer Set, a cross-trainer sneaker designed by Gabby and Nike's creative director. Her second shoe is called the Air Trainer Patrol.

Gabrielle Reece
c/o Jane Kachmer Management
5111 Ocean Front Walk, #4
Marina Del Rey, CA 90292

# Jerry Rice

*J*erry Rice has proven himself to be the best wide receiver ever to play professional football, holding nearly every major all-time receiving record. He can break a game wide open, going deep or evading tacklers to turn a short pass into a long gain. In college, Jerry had a great career playing for little known Mississippi Valley State University. He entered the NFL as a virtual unknown, but quickly made a name for himself with the San Francisco 49ers. Some may ask if he would have had as great a professional career if he hadn't played with quarterbacks as talented as Joe Montana and Steve Young. But perhaps the question should be: Would Montana and Young have *been* such great quarterbacks without Jerry Rice?

## Birthday Beat
*October 13, 1962*

74

## Cool Credits

➤ Named wide receiver on *The Sporting News* college all-American team, 1984
➤ Played in Super Bowl, 1989, 1990, 1995
➤ Holds NFL single-season record for most touchdown receptions (twenty-two), 1987
➤ Holds NFL career record for most touchdown receptions (118+), 1985–1995
➤ Selected for Pro Bowl ten consecutive years

## Vital Stats

➤ Height: 6'2"
➤ Weight: 190
➤ Full name: Jerry Lee Rice
➤ Birthplace: Starkville, Mississippi
➤ College: Mississippi Valley State University

➤ High School: B.L. Moor, in Crawford, Mississippi
➤ Current residence: San Francisco, California
➤ In his spare time: spends time with his family, plays golf, rides his Harley-Davidson motorcycle

### So You Want to Know—

How Jerry Rice first learned to catch tough passes? When he was a kid growing up in Starksville, Mississippi, his first job was working for his father, a bricklayer. Jerry would stay on the scaffold while his father and brother threw bricks up to him.

Jerry Rice
c/o Sports Management Group
222 S. Central, Suite 1008
St. Louis, MO 63105

# David Robinson

**D**avid Robinson has the perfect body and mind to play basketball—he's tall, lean, and very strong. Most importantly, he's very determined and patient. In fact, without such perseverance, David may not have made it to the NBA. In 1987, the San Antonio Spurs drafted him as their number-one pick, but David couldn't join them because he was committed to completing his military service in the United States Navy. David waited two full seasons, continuing to practice on his own, before he was finally able to put on an NBA uniform. Now, David's days of waiting are over. In 1995, he became the league's Most Valuable Player and his team, the Spurs, achieved the best record in basketball.

## Cool Credits

➤ NCAA Player of the Year, 1987
➤ First overall draft pick in NBA draft, 1987
➤ NBA Rookie of the Year, 1990
➤ IBM Award, for all-around contributions to team's success, 1990, 1991, 1994
➤ Olympic gold medal, 1992
➤ Led NBA with 4.49 blocked shots per game, 1992
➤ NBA leading scorer, 1994
➤ NBA Most Valuable Player, 1995

## So You Want to Know—

About David's musical pursuits? His love of music shows in his desire to learn new instruments even without a tutor. After he signed with the Spurs, he purchased a baby grand piano and then taught himself to play Beethoven sonatas. David is also learning to play the saxophone.

## Vital Stats

➤ Height: 7'1"
➤ Weight: 235
➤ Birthplace: Key West, Florida
➤ College: Naval Academy
➤ Current residence: San Antonio, Texas
➤ Nickname: The Admiral
➤ In his spare time: plays piano, goes cycling, plays golf
➤ Favorite food: lasagna

## Birthday Beat

*August 6, 1965*

• • • • • • • • • • • • • • • • • • • • • • • • • • • • •

David Robinson
c/o The Robinson Group
8632 Fredricksburg Rd., Suite 209
San Antonio, TX 78240

**77**

• • • • • • • • • • • • • • • • • • • • • • • • • • • • •

# Gabriela Sabatini

▼▼▼▼▼▼▼▼▼▼▼▼▼▼▼▼▼▼▼▼▼▼

*G*rowing up, Gabriela Sabatini remembers doing little other than playing tennis. "Tennis was like a toy to me," she says. "Instead of having dolls I was playing tennis." But being a tennis star was more than a childhood fantasy. At age ten she was the number-one-ranked player in Argentina in the girls twelve-and-under division. At fifteen, she turned pro and defeated six top-ranked pros during her first *month* on the tour. Today, she plays a mean baseline game with an awesome topspin on her forehand and backhand shots; she can lob the ball up or attack the net. Gabriela is the ultimate well-rounded player. She can do it all!

**Birthday Beat**
*May 16, 1970*

## Cool Credits

➤ Finalist at Hilton Head, South Carolina, upsetting three Top 10 players, Zina Garrison (#9), Pam Shriver (#8), and Manuela Maleeva (#5), 1985
➤ U.S. Open winner, 1990
➤ Wimbledon finalist, 1991
➤ Pan-Pacific Open Winner, 1992
➤ Top 10 ranking, 1986–1994

## Vital Stats

➤ Height: 5'8"
➤ Weight: 130
➤ Birthplace: Buenos Aires, Argentina
➤ Current residences: Buenos Aires and Key Biscayne, Florida
➤ Turned pro: 1985

### So You Want to Know—

Who Gabriela endorses in commercials? Ray-Ban sunglasses, Perrier bottled spring water, Fuji film, and Pepsi-Cola. There's even a perfume named after her called "Gaby," and it's as popular as she is.

➤ Nickname: Gaby
➤ In her spare time: enjoys singing, and playing cards, soccer, and video games
➤ Favorite food: Argentinian
➤ Famous relative: brother Osvaldo, Jr., a TV star in Buenos Aires

Gabriela Sabatini
c/o ProServ, Inc.
1101 W. Wilson Blvd., Suite 1800
Arlington, VA 22209

# Pete Sampras

*W*hen he was a kid, Pete wanted to be like Rod Laver, the legendary Australian tennis star who won eleven Grand Slam titles during the 1960s. As with most childhood dreams, the odds were pretty slim that he would ever become that great—or that he would ever even make it as a professional tennis player. He started playing when he was seven and still had a two-handed backhand shot when he was sixteen years old. Even at age seventeen, when Pete turned pro, it seemed unlikely that he would last (he was ranked 311). Two years later he became the youngest player ever to win the 1990 U.S. Open. Pete's philosophy was always to challenge himself and work on his weaknesses, even if that meant losing some matches along the way. He knew winning would follow eventually if he became the best tennis player *he* could be. And it did!

## Vital Stats

➤ Height: 6'1"
➤ Weight: 170

➤ Birthplace: Washington D.C.
➤ Current residence: Tampa, Florida
➤ Turned pro: 1988
➤ In his spare time: plays golf

## Cool Credits

➤ Compiled record of 70–18 and won five titles in seven finals, 1992

➤ Named IBM/ATP Tour Player of the Year, 1993, 1994

➤ Won U.S. Open, 1990, 1993

➤ Ranked Top 10, 1990–1995

➤ Won Wimbledon, 1993, 1994

➤ Ranked number one every week from September 1993 to September 1994, becoming the first player to hold this top position for an entire calendar year since Ivan Lendl in 1987

## Birthday Beat

*August 12, 1971*

### So You Want to Know—

How Pete's parents are affected by his fame? Sam and Georgia Sampras are Pete's number-one fans and have been very supportive of his career. But when Pete plays, his folks can't bear to watch, whether it's in person or on TV. They say it's too nerve-racking.

Pete Sampras
c/o International Management Group
22 E. 71st St.
New York, NY 10021

# Barry Sanders

arry Sanders is one of the most explosive running backs since Walter Payton. In fact, in Barry's rookie season, upon seeing Sanders play, Payton declared, "I don't know if I was ever *that* good." In the wink of an eye Barry can turn a seemingly busted play into a touchdown.

In college, he won the prestigious Heisman Trophy. He then became a player for the Detroit Lions, taking only five seasons to become their all-time leading rusher. But as good as he is, Barry is modest about his talent. Unlike many football stars who spike the ball or do a flamboyant dance after scoring a touchdown, Barry simply hands the ball to the nearest official and jogs back to the sideline to get ready for his next turn on the field.

**Birthday Beat**
*July 16, 1968*

82

## So You Want to Know—

How dedicated Barry Sanders is to his religion? Barry is a devout Christian who believes that a real man is a man of God. He conducts chapel services on game day mornings and weekly Bible study classes for his teammates.

## Vital Stats

➤ Height: 5'8"
➤ Weight: 203
➤ Birthplace: Wichita, Kansas
➤ College: Oklahoma State
➤ Current residence: Rochester Hills, Michigan
➤ 40-yard-dash speed: 4.27 seconds
➤ In his spare time: watches and plays basketball, reads
➤ Idol growing up: boxer Muhammad Ali
➤ Amount of weight he can squat lift: 557 pounds

## Cool Credits

➤ Oklahoma State record for touchdowns, fifty-six college career touchdowns, 1988
➤ Five touchdowns in the Holiday Bowl, 1988
➤ Heisman Trophy winner (best player in college football), 1988
➤ NFL Rookie of the Year, 1989
➤ Led NFC in rushing (1,470 yards), 1989, 1990
➤ Started in the Pro Bowl in each of his first five pro seasons

Barry Sanders
c/o David Ware and Associates
1800 Century Blvd. NE, Suite 950
Atlanta, GA 30345

# Deion Sanders

*T*here have been other two-sport athletes—most notably Bo Jackson, who
also played both baseball and football—but none have accomplished as
much in two sports as Deion Sanders. In
1992, he played with the Atlanta Braves in
his first World Series. In 1995, he played
in—and helped win—his first Super Bowl
with the San Francisco 49ers. As a baseball
player, he's developed into a premier hitter,
a solid fielder, and one of the most danger-
ous base-stealing threats. As a defensive
back on the gridiron, he's tough, fast, quick,
and can cover any receiver in the league.

## Cool Credits

➤ All-American defensive
back at Florida State
University, 1986–1988
➤ Jim Thorpe Award in
recognition of two-sport
athletes, 1988
➤ Named kick returner
on NFL all-pro team, 1992
➤ Led the National
League in triples
(fourteen), 1992
➤ Hit .533 for the Atlanta
Braves in the World
Series, 1992
➤ Super Bowl victory,
1995

## Vital Stats

➤ Height: 6'1"
➤ Weight: 195
➤ Full name: Deion
Luwynn Sanders
➤ Hometown: Fort
Meyers, Florida
➤ College: Florida State
University

## So You Want to Know—

How Deion stayed out of trouble when he was a kid? He avoided violence on the streets by getting involved in any sport he could. He grew up in a rough neighborhood in Fort Meyers, Florida. "There were a lot of drugs and gang violence around," says Deion. "I pretty much stayed out of it, although some of my best friends from home are in jail—and won't be out for a while."

➤ Current residence: Alpharetta, Georgia
➤ Nickname: Prime Time
➤ In his spare time: likes fishing and composing rap music
➤ Favorite food: fried lobster
➤ Idol growing up: Dr. Martin Luther King, Jr.

### Birthday Beat
*August 9, 1967*

Deion Sanders
c/o The San Francisco 49ers
4949 Centennial Blvd.
Santa Clara, CA 95054

# Emmitt Smith

## Cool Credits

➤ All-American, 1988–1990
➤ University of Florida all-time career rushing record (3,928 yards), as well as fifty-seven other school records
➤ Became the fifth leading all-time rusher in SEC history, 1990
➤ Led NFC in rushing, 1991–1993
➤ NFL Most Valuable Player, 1993
➤ Super Bowl MVP, 1993

## Birthday Beat

*May 15, 1969*

## So You Want to Know—

How Emmitt celebrated his twenty-fifth birthday? Emmitt invited about 1,000 guests and raised $25,000 for the I Have A Dream Foundation, an organization devoted to helping underprivileged kids achieve their dreams. Now that Emmitt has achieved his own dream—being a Super Bowl MVP—he says, "I'm going to help the dreams of some others come true by being an MVP off the field, too."

*H*e is the most consistent running back in the game. As a high school, college, and professional football player, Emmitt Smith has never had a bad season. When the Dallas Cowboys need a short yardage first down, they can count on Emmitt. When they need an explosive run up the middle, they can count on Emmitt. When they need a reception out of the backfield, they can count on Emmitt. For most running backs, a 1,000-yard season is an outstanding accomplishment, but for Emmitt, it's just average.

## Vital Stats

➤ Height: 5'9"
➤ Weight: 209
➤ Hometown: Escambia, Florida
➤ College: University of Florida
➤ Current residence: Pensacola, Florida
➤ In his spare time: runs his marketing firm, works toward his degree in therapeutic recreation, builds model railroads
➤ Number of football awards he received in 1993: more than seventeen!
➤ Favorite foods: anything his mom makes, especially lasagna

• • • • • • • • • • • • • • • • • • • • • • • • • • • •

Emmitt Smith
c/o Emmitt Inc.
3300 N. Pace Blvd., Store #210
Pensacola, FL 32505

# Picabo Street

□ □ □ □ □ □ □ □ □ □ □ □ □ □ □ □ □

*D*ownhill skiing may not be the most popular sport around, but it is certainly one of the most exciting. At its forefront is an excellent skier with a very cool name: Picabo [PEEK-a-boo] Street. She hasn't always been such a successful skier, though. In 1990, when her career was just starting, she was sent home by the head coach of the U.S. women's ski team, Paul Major. He wasn't sure if Picabo had the commitment to become a great ski racer. She had allowed herself to get out of shape and had developed a bad attitude. Picabo learned her lesson and re-dedicated herself and her passion. Ever since, she has been downhill skiing like a rocket with new determination and an amazing talent.

## Cool Credits

➤ Won the North American Championship Series (NorAm) overall title, 1991, 1992

➤ First Place in World Cup DH (downhill) I, Lake Louise, Albania, 1994

➤ First Place in World Cup DH II, Cortina, Italy, 1995

➤ First Place in World Cup DH, Are, Sweden, 1995

➤ First Place in World Cup DH, Saalbach, Austria, 1995

➤ First Place in World Cup DH, Lenzerheide, Switzerland, 1995

➤ First Place in World Cup DH, Bormio, Italy, 1995
➤ Became first U.S. skier to win a World Cup downhill title, 1995

## Vital Stats

➤ Height: 5'7"
➤ Weight: 143
➤ Birthplace: Triumph, Idaho
➤ Current residence: Sun Valley, Idaho

➤ Major influence: Paul Major, her coach
➤ Collects: troll dolls (she has a troll attached to one of her ski hats)

## Birthday Beat

*April 3, 1971*

## So You Want to Know—

About Picabo's unusual name? She explains, "My mom and dad were hippie parents. They moved to Sun Valley in '67 and along the way they drove through this small town of Picabo. Dad thought it was a cool name and might be good for a kid. Mom went to a library and read about the Picabo Indians who lived in southern Idaho. Well, they liked the name."

Picabo Street
c/o U.S. Ski Team
P.O. Box 100
Park City, UT 84060

# Frank Thomas

▼▼▼▼▼▼▼▼▼▼▼▼▼▼▼▼▼▼▼▼

*F*rank Thomas is one of the most feared sluggers in baseball. A hulking 257 pounds of solid muscle, this Chicago White Sox player makes pitchers think twice about grooving one down the middle. White Sox broadcaster Ken Harrelson once said, "Someday soon we will see a team intentionally walk Frank with the bases loaded . . . And when they do I will stand up and applaud them for their intelligence."

During his rookie season, Frank was named Player of the Week twice and Player

 of the Month once by his league. In fact, Frank is not only a powerful hitter, but a smart one. In his first two major league seasons, he led the American League in walks, proving he knows how to recognize a good pitch.

**Birthday Beat**
*May 27, 1968*

## Cool Credits

➤ American League MVP, 1993, 1994

➤ Broke a White Sox record for walks (138), 1991

➤ Posted triple crown stats (the best in his league in each category) with a .353 batting average, 101 RBIs and 38 home runs, 1994 (prior to the season-ending strike in August)

➤ Joined Hall-of-Famers Ted Williams and Lou Gehrig as the only players to get at least 20 home runs, 100 RBIs, 100 runs scored, and 100 walks while hitting .300 or better in four consecutive seasons, 1994

### So You Want to Know—

How Frank keeps all the praise from going to his head? Since he became a major leaguer, Frank has kept his own personal motto taped above his locker. It reads simply "DBTH" and stands for "Don't Believe the Hype."

## Vital Stats

➤ Height: 6'5"
➤ Weight: 257
➤ Birthplace: Columbus, Georgia
➤ College: Auburn University
➤ Current residence: Chicago, Illinois
➤ Nickname: The Big Hurt

Frank Thomas
c/o The Chicago White Sox
New Comiskey Park
333 W. 35th St.
Chicago, IL 60616

# Reggie White

**B**eing a lineman in football is like being on the front lines of a war. It's an all-out battle of strength, endurance, and pain, and when the big plays are made, the credit rarely goes to the linemen. As a result, there aren't a lot of famous defensive linemen. But Reggie White has managed to make a name for himself. First with Memphis in the USFL (United States Football League) and later as a Philadelphia Eagle and Green Bay Packer, Reggie has become one of the most feared defensive linemen in the NFL. His combination of strength, agility, and speed has made him one of the premier sack artists in football. He's also a great defender against the run and is extremely tough and durable. In his entire NFL career, he has never missed a game due to injury, although plenty of quarterbacks and running backs have missed games due to *his* hard hits.

## Birthday Beat
*December 19, 1961*

## Vital Stats
➤ Height: 6'5"
➤ Weight: 295
➤ Birthplace: Chattanooga, Tennessee
➤ College: Tennessee

➤ Current residence: Maryville, Tennessee
➤ Nickname: Big Dog, The Minister of Defense
➤ Favorite athlete: Michael Jordan
➤ Idols growing up: former 76er stars Julius Erving and Bobby Jones

## Cool Credits

➤ All-state in high school basketball and football, 1979
➤ Selected to *Parade* magazine's all-American football team, 1979
➤ Most sacks in NFL history (137)
➤ Can run the 40-yard dash in under five seconds

### So You Want to Know—

What Reggie's other passion is? The reason he is called the Minister of Defense is because preaching is his other vocation. Reggie is a Baptist minister, and after he retires from football, he plans to deliver sermons full time. For now, he's content delivering grief to NFL quarterbacks.

Reggie White
c/o The Green Bay Packers
1265 Lombardi Ave.
Green Bay, WI 54307

93

# Steve Young

□ □ □ □ □ □ □ □ □ □ □ □ □ □ □ □ □ □ □

*S*teve Young has been the highest rated quarterback for the past four seasons, and when he's hot he is truly unstoppable. He is easily the best running quarterback in the game; every year he leads quarterbacks in yards rushed. In or out of the pocket, he can throw with great accuracy, hardly ever tossing an interception. For years he was overshadowed by Joe Montana, who is perhaps the greatest quarterback of all time, but now Joe is gone and, with his 1995 Super Bowl performance, Steve has proven that he is up to the task of leading the San Francisco 49ers.

**Birthday Beat**
*October 11, 1961*

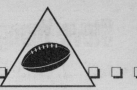

## Cool Credits

➤ NCAA all-American, 1983
➤ Heisman Trophy runner-up, 1983
➤ Played with 49ers in Super Bowl victories, 1989, 1990, 1995
➤ NFL Most Valuable Player, 1992, 1995
➤ NFL's highest rated quarterback four seasons in a row (an NFL record), 1991–1994

## Vital Stats

➤ Height: 6'2"
➤ Weight: 205
➤ Birthplace: Salt Lake City, Utah
➤ College: Brigham Young University
➤ Current residence: Palo Alto, California
➤ In his spare time: plays golf, enjoys movies and skiing

➤ Favorite food: Italian
➤ Idol growing up: Hall-of-Famer Roger Staubach
➤ Favorite band: 10,000 Maniacs
➤ Secret ambition: to climb Mt. Everest

### So You Want to Know—

What kind of athlete Steve was as a youngster? He remembers being the last player chosen in pickup football games. In high school he once threw *seven* interceptions in one game! And his first year at Brigham Young University, he was the *eighth* string quarterback.

Steve Young
c/o The San Francisco 49ers
4949 Centennial Blvd.
Santa Clara, CA 95054

# Photo Credits

**Cover:** Jerry Rice, Mike Powell/Allsport Photography USA; Hakeem Olajuwan, Steve Granitz/Retna; Steffi Graf, Pat Garcia/Retna; Eric Lindros, Robert Laberge/ Allsport Photography USA